Jesus Teaches How to Pray

Sinclair Ferguson

This series looks at the teachings of Jesus.
Read the story and discuss the pictures.

Illustrated by Jeff Anderson

Published by Christian Focus Publications, Geanies House, Fearn,
Tain, Ross-shire, IV20 1TW, Scotland.
© Copyright 2004 Sinclair Ferguson
www.christianfocus.com   Printed in the United Kingdom

One of the things that amazed Jesus' disciples was this: Jesus loved to pray. Jesus wants us to be able to tell God, our heavenly Father, everything about ourselves.

And he wants us to know that our Heavenly Father is so great and good that he listens to our prayers. That is why Jesus taught his disciples what we call 'The Lord's Prayer'.

Sometimes it seems quite easy to pray. But at other times we feel sleepy and lazy, or we can't think what to say. Sometimes we don't want to pray.

Jesus – as always – can help us. When Jesus prayed he was really talking to God as his Father. He really knew and loved God. It was amazing to hear him pray.

The Lord Jesus wants his disciples to be able to pray the way he did. So, in his famous Sermon on the Mount, he taught us how to speak to the Heavenly Father.

He gave us a kind of outline prayer, to help us see the things we should talk to God about.

Do you know how to do jig-saw puzzles? First of all you put together the pieces that go round the edge. Then it is much easier to fill it in.

Jesus has given us an outline prayer. We can fill it in with our own prayers.

When we pray to God as our Father, we can tell him that we know he is good.

That is just like telling him that we love him very much.

What should we ask for, first of all? Jesus taught that God's kingdom had come near. Well, we can pray that God's kingdom – his reign – will be seen all over the world.

God's will is always done in heaven. We can pray that it will be done on earth too.

That is saying that we want to do our Heavenly Father's will. Is that what you want? Do you want to do God's will?

The Father cares about us. He knows that we need his help very much indeed. How can we ask him for what we really need? What are the things that we really need?

The wonderful thing about the way Jesus teaches us to pray is that he knows exactly what we really need.

We think we need lots and lots of things. But Jesus says we only need a few things.

First we need food and clothes and things like that.

That's why Jesus says we should ask God to give us what we need each day.

Second, we need to remember that we have sinned. In fact we are like people who can't pay what we owe.

We call that being a debtor. There is no way we can repay the debt we owe to God. Jesus says: 'Ask God to cancel the debts of your sins!'

Third, Jesus teaches us to remember that we are weak. We don't have the power to fight against temptation. We can't overcome the Devil in our own strength. So we need to ask God to protect us.

If you ever find it hard to pray, remember the outline Jesus has given you. Begin with one of the things he tells us to pray about.

Think about what that means. Then you will begin to speak to the Heavenly Father about other things too.

Our Father in heaven,
hallowed be your name,
your kingdom come,
your will be done
on earth as it is
in heaven.
Give us today
our daily bread.
Forgive us
our debts,
as we also
have forgiven
our debtors.
And lead us
not into
temptation,
but deliver us
from the evil one.
Amen.

Do you speak to God? Do you know what you need? Have you asked him to forgive your sins?

You can read about Jesus' outline prayer in Matthew 6:5-15.